THE NEW SERIES   #79   AHSAHTA PRESS   BOISE, IDAHO   2017

I believe nonetheless that I am present in your thoughts. I spoke of you several times today. I meant it as

He stood
in the doorway. He sat here.
And the window
was open.

was a go

The End of S

KATE GREENSTREET

remember landscape?
It used to be everywhere.

o,k

a kind of blessing. Is a secret always a promise? And does a promise always foretell the end of something?

AHSAHTA PRESS
Boise State University, Boise, Idaho 83725
Cover design: M+K Greenstreet
Book design: Kate Greenstreet and Janet Holmes
Printed in Canada

LIBRARY OF CONGRESS CATALOGING-IN-PUBLICATION DATA
Names: Greenstreet, Kate, author.
Title: The end of something / Kate Greenstreet.
Description: Boise, Idaho : Ahsahta Press/Boise State University, [2017] |
    Series: The new series ; #79
Identifiers: LCCN 2017029601 | ISBN 9781934103746 (softcover : acid-free
    paper) | ISBN 1934103748 (softcover : acid-free paper)
Classification: LCC PS3607.R4666 A6 2017 | DDC 813/.6—dc23
LC record available at https://lccn.loc.gov/2017029601

ACKNOWLEDGMENTS
The End of Something includes some work from several chapbooks: *Learning the Language* (Etherdome Press), *Rushes* (above/ground press), *Statues* (Big Game Press), and *This is why I hurt you* (Lame House Press). Poems in this book have also appeared in a WinteRed Press chaplet and in the anthologies *Letters to the World* (Red Hen Press), *Fire on Her Tongue* (Two Sylvias Press), *As if it Fell from the Sun* (Etherdome Press), and *Ligatures: poets of France and America* (Catala Press). Many thanks to the editors of those books and presses, and to the editors of *Fact-Simile,* the publishers of *The Correspondence Project,* and the editors of *Arsenic Lobster, Barrow Street, Bird Dog, BOAAT, can we have our ball back?, Court Green, Gramma, Delirious Hem, Denver Quarterly, DREGINALD, The Duplications, The Dusie Tuesday Poem, Edison Literary Review, Everyday Genius, GutCult, Laurel Review, LIT, Loose Change, Map Literary, Massachusetts Review, Northern New England Review, The Offending Adam, Ping-Pong, Pool, spacecraftprojects, Sugar House Review, Sweet, TAB, Tammy, The Tiny, Touch the Donkey, Tupelo Quarterly, Under a Warm Green Linden, Verse Daily,* and *Waxwing,* where parts of *The End of Something* have appeared.

My biggest thanks, as always, to Janet Holmes.

I dreamed I was a
thousand years old
and then, when I woke up,
I was a thousand years old
and I thought: am I dreaming?

There's always that moment with people,
right? You look back . . . you can't believe

how they just don't love you.
And how, in the minute before that,
you didn't know.

There was a place, near water.
The people had come from somewhere else
and settled. How we came to exist.
How we came to be here, everywhere at once.

How could I say nothing?

Well, it's a long walk ahead.

For a long time,
I didn't know.

And it's all just another story
about how life could be.

A psychic told me once I had the mind of a nun. As if there would be only one kind, for nuns. The offices of seers we consulted in the South sometimes had chickens. The vestibules were swimming with the poor—bobbing, drowning, in our lake of dreams and wishes.

Tell me everything you want to do while there's still time.

Keep in touch.

1. WHAT IT MEANS TO BE A STRANGER

This is a map of where we are.
The silhouetted shapes of people
and animals. There's a little bit of color.

I saw him for a minute.

He touched the edge
of the life we knew. Color
and the lack of color.

He put the wound out there, in the granite.
For some reason, I locked the door.

—It was dark?

—It was night.

It's hard to resist the urge
to keep a fire going.

Even when you're not cold anymore.

Even when you're burning
up what you might need later.

2. OF WHAT WILL NOT REACH US UNTIL MORNING

Is he inside? He is.

He's testing himself.
He uses music.

A small scattering of crickets.

A foreseeable
loss.

Fourteen years in Chicago.

I went halfway and turned around.

There's Franny's house again.

3. LEAVES FELL

He wasn't born blind.
He had witnessed an
accident.

They were boys,
they were vulnerable.
That didn't make them good.

—Does he hope for justice?

—How do you solve *your* problems?

4. I AM WRITING THIS IN THE DARK

Did she lock it? Or was it locked?
My life has changed since we last spoke.

No resting. No tuning.
But I want to keep the room, and the chair.

We loved blue.
That's intimacy, isn't it?

She was always happy.
I've been thinking

of Thoreau, and feeling the desire to walk.
To walk for hours a day, as we used to.

5. PEOPLE WHO ARE MIKE, PEOPLE WHO KNOW MIKE, AND PEOPLE WHO JUST MET MIKE

You can be anywhere and you start bleeding

Or the sky
"ghosting"

The day I met him
I never thought twice

I never had a chance

I'd be standing at the top of the stairs
in a trench coat

I would be a travel
agent

Not only that, his name was . . . oh god,
I did date him . . .

"none known"
Like smoke

another night of
"These rooms is"

and we will have all
kinds of room

and this is
special ground—just for this purpose

"special thanks" but really it's
"what child is this?"

6. HERMES IS THE GOD OF THE ROADS .

Michael came to where I was living.
Storm home? Don't think so.
The wall was actually removed.
I was so glad to see him.

He was tall, he was wearing a green jacket.
Laid our main. You want to know about our life
in the body? Know how to stop?

Leave space between the dead and "I thought."
We have chosen the theme of peace.

Be there, dropping. Dropping like a small cloud of birds: three, eight, twelve, fifteen hundred men. Michael came to where I was living. He brought a pizza, he was letting the dog eat it with him. "Be there," like they say, "for us."

We don't even know if we're getting the good stuff. Blinds closed, bed unmade at three. We have chosen. The challenge was "to work with."

Michael came to where I was living, walking on the railing. We chose the theme of balance.

Short answer? No movement from the plot.

I wanted him to tell me the secret of what I should be doing now. He was going to.

But we never got around to it.

Things collect around a man, let you notice: who's at the center. We had chosen the theme "ghost" but were having second thoughts.

Michael won't cut the reason why. Knows the river names. Says: "But we're still young." Then says: "I'm kidding." The challenge was: "Things collect."

Souvenir: scrap of paper with the words "Coffee Jars" written in your hand. The hand that drew the angel with the hard-on, and the man who walked a cockroach on a leash. A hundred years have passed since we last spoke.

Five miles south, complete—see it from above: that beautiful blue snake. Can't be allowed to happen. Thoughts divined, and now the river changes.

Sometimes I feel like I'm *training* a snake. Find a steep, alternative route. We had chosen the theme "It would be more like this."

I was unable to transfer. I am a simple farmer. We had chosen the theme "The corners of the mouth."

Lead us to the mouth of the river. From the banks. Souvenir: the coffee can of change. Talk to us in tongues.

We have chosen the theme "I thought we were friends."

You know how sometimes when you're fishing and you bring up an old boot, you think: haven't I brought this boot up before? Haven't I gotten rid of it before?

Tell them: seaweed, blacktop, lilac. Rose of Sharon, not for the scent. This guy, his book is full of people but he's wandering alone. There's at least one more challenge.

Souvenir: the jar of river clay.

Keep moist with the water from the river. Keep stirred. Keep moving.

Michael came—I was so glad to see him. He was tall. I gave him a long hug. I wanted him to tell me the secret of what I should be doing now. He was going to. He'd brought a pizza, he was letting the dog eat it with him. He seemed so relaxed.

7. THIS IS A TRAVELING SONG

The escaped convict's story is a traveling story.
The language is full of gaps and problems of tense.

One time you asked for a sign and found a shell.
Add one minute for every thousand miles.

We learn to speak by hearing sounds
and deciding what they mean.
My father was alive, but he was tired.

Sensitive to distances, the dangers
of spring. Guessing
what lies beneath the ground.

What moves below the ground
What stirs
under the ground
Guessing about weather
Imagining the rooms

Some days finding glass,
mostly green. Blue is rare.
Add another minute.
Do they know we're here?

Learn the lesson of the pioneer.
Learn by losing.

Everybody's trying to get home.

We waited for the optimum conditions,
but in the end we set off in a storm.

1

I want to speak plainly, not un-include.

2

I have missed our conversation.

3

A few years ago something happened.

4

I spent a whole day writing you a letter.

5

I thought I'd made the most beautiful thing I ever made.

6

"Hermes is the god of the roads. He rules the ways in between,
the linking routes between different domains and levels of the
psyche. He presides over the wanderer and the merchant,

7

for he belongs nowhere and travels everywhere, speaking every
language and dealing in every currency."
(Liz Greene, in *The Luminaries*)

8. COLOR COMES FROM OUTSIDE

The shutter opens. She decides to walk.

I was on my way to spend the weekend
with friends. I decided to walk.

What can you tell us about the town?

The shutters opened. What I'm saying is
I came down the stairs.

He was sitting at the kitchen table.

Here are his books. Handwritten.

This story
and the next one—

it's called "falling into a new consciousness."

9. HE WAS A BOY ONCE

He stands, his fingers graze the table

His fingers spread
like a rake

His nose, longer
when he's under stress

As when he says "Fear gets us nowhere"
an obvious untruth, since here we are

His hat is made of bread

The bottle breaks—a collection of cells.

Just across the river, the trees turning green.
Just say

she will meet a trusted person.

Sometimes understanding
skips a generation.

And then how sad—to see a photo like that?

He'd waited all day to do
what he came to do.

10. DREAM ABOUT BEING A GIRL

I'm supposed to be in a wedding. I am the bride. I have my white dress all ready but at the last minute I have to go to a funeral instead. I wear a black dress with a wide belt and a short black wig. It's still 1968.

We're at the funeral mass. I'm afraid to go up to communion by myself but my grandmother is going, so I follow her. As we get close to the altar, I notice that everyone kneeling there is male. Gran slips into a pew, leaving me alone in the aisle. I try to leave through a hidden panel door. Luckily it works.

Outside, I see a girl who looks familiar. She says, maliciously: "Did you buy that wig for the funeral?" I don't answer. It seems to me that she should know why I have the wig on.

11. THE PUPIL

A genius! they say. Or then,
she has almost no gifts.

Get the pipe in
and bury it.
What we began to know,
we began to know in secret.
We thought the future
had arrived. Fields, a stony place,
then forest. All positions
being apparent, no one agrees
about what happened next.
It was the past. Shoe
that fits.
Mathematics
was a prayer they did
with chalk.

I pondered the meaning
of the letters—thx, lowercase,
period—instead of thanks.
Decided I had said too much. I waited
to be asked. Shoe that fits, shoe
made of glass.
Begins to explain
how in prayer
the soul is united with God.

Describes how we may know we are not
mistaken about this.

They have very long days, standing around. A lot of chewing. It always seems to be summer, the flies, or else it rains.

Like us, they make the days from the hours that are given. They appreciate punctuality. They show up on time. If you're late, they look at you. A terrible look—as if, for once, they're going to try to understand you.

They have a bony, hairy part on their face. The top of their head would have horns. They're really different from each other, but they have a lot in common.

I could tell you so much about cows! Their giant toenails. And how, while still very young, they begin to wait for something. Soon they seem to accept that it won't ever come. But they keep waiting. What we imagine is their sadness is this perfect, hopeless waiting.

I've watched a single cow standing in a field a thousand times. They have no respite, just the grass. The mother acts detached, almost indifferent to the calf after it's born—but when it's taken away, they begin to call each other. They look for each other with their voices, and everybody knows it's wrong.

It takes something like 345 squirts to get a gallon of milk. You get three or four gallons a milking, depends on the cow. She needs to be milked twice a day, morning and night, no matter what.

When a cow is moved to a different field, the milk changes flavor. When they shit, it falls from a distance and, in a cold barn, steam rises off it. You can see the breath come and go through their immense nostrils.

If you're a child when you see a calf born, you always know there's a place as big as you inside a cow.

I think people don't love them more because they don't do all that pet pretending. But when they're in their stanchion, you can't resist laying a hand flat on their side, even though all you get back is the rough switch of tail when you least expect it.

Did I mention how they can shift slightly, and push you—up against the hay bales when the barn gets full—and they don't notice.

13. ONE BLACK LEAF

What was your mother's name?

14. THIS MUST BE THE PLACE

We visited a house I used to live in.
Bright grass was growing in the rooms.
Early morning, summer.

Why have we come?

Pages ripped from a book.
He's throwing money from the bridge.
It's an actual expression:

"Change blindness." Meaning,
you don't notice there's a change.

Light on two sides. One great object.
Living "in," more secret than before.

In the evening she went down.
Everything I knew of evermore.

8
It's a big book. It's big, and long.

9
We carry it around.

10
The reason we're here.

11
"There is a secret place. A radiant sanctuary. As real as your own kitchen." (Teresa of Ávila, *Interior Castle*)

12
You don't have to know anything
to talk about something you see.

13
"Consequently, what haunts are not the dead,

14
but the gaps left within us by the secrets of others."
(Nicolas Abraham, "Notes on the Phantom")

15. INTROVERT

Deep in my own green element,
I met a friend.
My double, my dearest.

Others
pulled me out of the sea,
placed me

in this pan of water,
added salt
and taught me to eat bread.

16. BRIGHT GRASS

One tree in the field. But that's nice.

She always comes the same way home.
Palms black
from handling the coins,

certain walls, certain words, weathers.

Some people use a sentence.
Trying to right a wrong
in the mind.

They think, because it's happened
before

They believe they're stronger
(numbers)

Actually, she didn't have
She didn't go
We took her down

Have you ever
been held down?
I really don't know.

I've seen a dog swim out there half a mile.
Sayin' the dog's smarter than you?

Throw it in and forget it.

Far enough. It's always nice
to get home.

Nice to see her looking so beautiful.

17. BLACK PALMS

She was always taking pictures.
By the bridge. Waiting. She waited
so long.

Darkness, he could see nothing
in front or behind him. Mountains.
What else?

There are not many
pictures of him.
She really wants to lie down.

18. TRACKS

In the dream I slept all night and you were a saint,
your shirt stained yellow near the heart, spontaneously
blue under the arms.

Turns out to be music, our prayers.
We went to tell our mother in her bulb-lit grotto.
Chipping
a little, but she still looks great,
her arms outstretched and her veil,
refuge of sinners, cause of our joy.

Wisdom had built herself a house in the dream. I was
twins, I was looking for something.

Well, I grew up with him, you know. His personality was problematic but his suffering was compelling. I don't think about him that much anymore. I had a glow-in-the-dark statue of him as a child. I mean, when I was a child. It glowed sort of green, very soothing. I wonder if they still make those. All the rooms had paper drapes. And plastic armchairs—yellow, or red. Cheerful. Blonde night-tables and dressers, "Danish," the same in every room.

20. WHO'S YOUR LITTLE FRIEND?

Sometimes you sleep well, sometimes not at all.
dabchick, the little grebe, the pie-billed grebe

I had another little doll not my real one.

I was drinking my milk
and there was a little tooth
in it and I thought: What's that?
Is that a little tooth?

I felt around in my mouth, but it wasn't mine. It was
tiny. And I thought: He's murdering the innocents.

The innocence? It's a dream I'm having.

Shhh . . . I can help you. If you've done wrong.
My bed is right here. Let's lie down.

21. DISAPPEARING TWIN

Like Jesus said: "Be separate."
You do it in your head.

Mathematics?
It's green inside.
Translucent.
It has flecks.
The light comes in
in shapes.
It's so soothing.
Safe.
It doesn't get hot
and when there's rain,
it makes a nice sound,
a patting sound.
The water collects
in the curves.

Everybody likes the mild light.
There's only one chair.

15

Unerase the distance.

16

It must be a dream because I see myself

17

from the back. In a better world, we'd all be doing more.

18

Proverbs 9:1

19

He had a light, I had a pain that woke me.

20

Sometimes the person who's bad is the other person's only friend.

21

Some crazy tuning like B E B E B E. Capo first fret.

22. SPECIAL BLINDFOLD

—I was looking at the curtains, and behind them to the dark. You know, "the lonely detective."

—You identify with that?

—I do.

—How did you feel?

—I felt like I'd been in the past again.

—Missing-like?

—I was still a girl.

23. WE LOVED BLUE

I was lying in bed, picturing the parts
of the camera. We were both so cold.

Later, I told them I'd seen her
out by the lake.

24. LITTLE NUT

Once I was small, I was your child. Your chest was hard, shallow, like a walnut shell. I was your child.

I tapped your chest, I was an unopened walnut shell. Was there a nut inside? I tapped your chest.

Your chest was hard, it sounded hollow: was the nut inside? I was inside you once, when I was small.

25. THEORY OF THE QUALITIES OF SEEING

a point on the map / what is in us already

horizon / motel / what falls from the sky

mountain / maple leaf / world without end

broken dishes / house and tree

acorn / moon and stars

What am I carrying?

What was I running from?

What is the same the world over?

She could figure out problems. She liked chalk and black-boards and cleaning the erasers. She knew all the Roman numerals. Even the phrase, "Roman numerals" . . . like something from another life. People walking—trying to get somewhere, and you just don't. We're not really going anywhere—to France?

I wanted to see Einstein's house. I wanted to get into his backyard, really bad, but somebody lived there. You make a mistake, and it's mysterious. Making things up is a mistake—it's not true, it's not accurate.

The thing about erasing: the eraser was very big and your numbers were small. So you had to use the corner or you'd take away more than you meant to.

27. I KNOW A WAY OF BEING INVISIBLE

Let's pray together.
You wear this.

28. FINISH EACH DAY

Her dream was a ranch in Missouri.
People always mention this. Her dream.

As if she'd wake up in the morning and say to her man:
I had that dream again. The cattle, the fences, the sky . . .

—You've been in the same position now for nearly nine
hours, with your head at that angle and your knee up. I'm
afraid you'll be sore if you don't move around a little bit.

—Scrape off the math.

—Math?

—M-A-T-H

—What about the math?

—Get rid of it.

22

The ability to see or recall.

23

When the eyes are open or closed.

24

Attachment, memory, narrative.

25

Seeing best where you are looking.

26

If the child does not lose hope.

27

Where does the outside world begin?

28

Can I feel your marks?

Tracy had just moved and we went to see the house, out by itself in a huge cornfield. Her little girls were playing on the porch and one of them told me about the ghost who lived there, who was a little girl too. I didn't pay much attention. But later I saw a tiny ladder moving by itself, first this way, then that—and I knew it was the little ghost carrying it around. Which was spooky at first. But now I can see her, and she is so tiny and quiet and sweet—I really like her now.

How she got to be a ghost was that she ate a plate of spiders—a plate of plastic spiders that were meant to scare people, not to be eaten. The little sisters told me this.

30. THE LAWS OF ACORNS

I'm always looking.
What you wanted, I wanted that for you.

But you do what the man wants, don't you?

It's like how money
is based on gold.

This was someone's home. What happened
to these people?

It would be valuable to know.

31. M-A-T-H

She said she would come back if she could, to tell me. To say what it was like, but she didn't.

Snow blows off the roof in ghost shapes. Inside, the half-done puzzle, a cliché, hogs the table. Hundreds of tiny blue pieces for sky. Green for the hill, gray for clouds. In another pile, some of the shirts we wore. A few remarks that marked me. The mail arrives: catalogs, bills. I begin looking at mattress covers, to calm myself. I count in my own way.

Back in life, you said.

But you got sad.
Why?

I heard that little music,

dumped his hundred handwritten pages
and all the photographs from overseas.

All the soldiers,
the girls.
Once
in the heart.
More lists
of the things we'll need.
A close-up of apples.

Disappointment is an obstacle.

Said he was unusual, as a boy.
Then couldn't name the first thing about him.

Everything he thought was going to happen

we know about
from the songs.

Our respects.

Are you all alone?
You can make a wish.

—Do you consider it a science?

—Well, I'm not sure what the definition is. "Science" doesn't mean "this is true." It's almost the opposite, right? Because science is all about testing. So yeah, I'd say yeah.

—So you have this piece of paper with the two words written on it: "Mars" and "brother." What do they have to do with one another?

—You could say Mars represents masculine or aggressive forces in a personality. Mars rules Aries, the first sign of the zodiac. "I am" would be the sentence. It could represent the men in your life. The men in anybody's life. And whatever a person might think of as their man-ness.

—And "brother"?

—"He ain't heavy, he's my brother."

—How accurate is that?

—It happened. I think.

  Because all men are brothers.

—Also quoting someone?

—It's a song. "Because all men are brothers, wherever they
may be" [hums a little]

—When they said "men" they meant "humans" then?

—Who knows? Who knows . . . supposedly. But maybe
they just meant men. Am I my brother's keeper?

I'm just going to answer with quotations, apparently.

—There might be a reason why.

—Well, "brother" is always, by its nature, related to something else. It's a relationship word. "The family of man."

—How to serve man.

—Right, it's a cookbook. [slight smile]

—When you see the word Mars, what do you think of? Or when you hear the word Mars, what do you feel?

—Mars black.

—That's a feeling?

—It's a color.

—It's a shade of black?

—Yes. An earthy brownish black. Not a cold black, it's warm. But what do I think of? I think of war. I think of anger, energy, aggression. I think of men.

—Your first thought isn't of the planet itself.

—If you lived on Mars, would your blood boil?

—I assume the planets get progressively colder as they get further from the sun.

—I don't know. But I think your blood would boil.

I was on the toilet, bleeding. A TV was on, some ordinary story. People started coming in to watch it, sitting on some chairs and benches that I hadn't seen. I didn't want to show that I was bleeding, I tried to be discreet, but I was sitting in plain view. Then I remembered the two plastic bags I had with me, full of bloody rags. The bags were opaque—white bags from the food store—but the blood was showing through. I hoped no one would notice. I finished, wiped myself, picked up the bags, and tried to leave through a hidden panel door. Luckily it worked. This could be my talent. This could be my talent, if you'd recognize it.

Do you have a car?

35. DO YOU LIKE THIS MUSIC?

There's a tiny church down the highway.
A chapel and kitchen, one room. The organ
pedals are worn. The walls, sky blue.

Call it intuition.

The shutter
opens. "The problem of
consciousness" or, as of a ship, "laden."

29
This is what we were promised. The appearance of another body.

30
"For an acorn to undergo its latent possible transformation, it must begin to obey the laws of oak trees and gradually cease being an acorn at all." (Maurice Nicoll, *The New Man*)

31
That very night, I slept in her bed.

32
To answer the question, where we come from.

33
"Dear friend, I can believe in the influence of Mars as fully as I can in the aorta. It's all invisible, in a normal day—though felt, as rhythm or excitement or pressure."

34
Do we take them all with us? the people we've been?

35
Realized the blessing didn't need to touch my skin.

36. BEFORE THE BRIGHT FIRE

Like Jesus said: "Who can you lie to?"

Meaning,
who'll believe you?

My brother knows what he's doing.

People ask us for directions, but we don't
live here. We sat on benches twice today.

37. HE SAT HERE

I remember,
of course.
He was

as he was.
And myself,
yes.

The picture
is imperfect,
partial.

As when it's said:
"I am partial
to"

There was no name for it.
It was too early.

There was only so much
I could sort out.

—Mike? He has a lot of talent as a "people person." Not necessarily extroverted, but persuasive. The prototype in my life didn't have a lot of *natural* talent at anything else. He had some. He wrote and he painted. But I think he got discouraged that he wasn't great at anything right away. He loved music. If he'd had discipline, he might've done something. But he'd rather get high. I get it but, you know . . . He'd rather get high and take it off somebody else. "He'll take the eyes out of your head," as the Irish say, "and tell you you look better without them."

People like that, they can be funny. Or they're handsome, they're charming. Maybe they seem wounded in a way that makes you want to help, even when they're much more powerful than you are. And either they are this thing that everybody knows about now, I forget what you call it . . . a sociopath. Who has no empathy, no conscience, but has talents to make you believe that they care about things, and, you know, like any animal, they'll cry when kicked. Or they'll bare their teeth when kicked. They have "feelings," but that doesn't mean they can have a relationship with you, or anyone, in a normal way. If you care about them, if Mike is your brother, your lover, your father, you'll be *in* a relationship but he can't . . . You could say he's not fully human. I mean, everybody likes the not fully human guy or girl in the movies. But the not fully human person in life?

—It wears thin.

—It wears you out.

—So either he's a sociopath . . . or?

—Or he's not. And you don't know. And you *can't* know. He either keeps fooling you into thinking that he *is* fully human, or he is, but he's been badly hurt. He's been hurt in his youth, or maybe he's got a Cosmic Cross in his chart. He has obstacles, psychological obstacles greater than yours.

—Insurmountable?

—Not insurmountable maybe, but he'll need self-discipline. And luck. Now, Mike usually does have luck. He has luck, but it's not always good luck.

—You keep saying "he."

—Most Mikes I've known have been male. They're easier to spot, for me. And of course they're often named Mike. It's funny how that works.

39. WHAT FALLS FROM THE SKY

I understood certain words.

The word for why.
The word for always.
The word for speak.

That the truth means
what is going to happen. Or
what I must do.

We drink it down: "To death!"
He put the blanket on my head.
He said, "Sometimes, I think

you just want to disappear."

40. THEY ALL WANT TO TRY THE VEIL

He sat right here.
You had your turn, okay?

She seems unaware of him and in a kind of trance.
The stems are magnified by water.

41. -LESS

Meaning none.
(appears as lost)

"I'll raise my head like this."

42. THE LITTLE GHOST

She's like I used to be,
so quiet and good.

She waits for me.
She wants to tell me things.

36
I don't follow the news. I have to follow something else.

37
The way the field is different from a tree
And if a soldier should lay down his arms

38
Free will, the theory of: The belief that, given again the same
conditions, humans can choose to do otherwise than what they
did do.

39
They need two miracles.

40
"this movement toward something . . ."

41
The smallest measurable interval.

42
He says he sometimes hears you singing with your friend.

43. LAKE ROAD

Sometimes I see him out there.
With his dog.

Here's the girl he wants to meet.

Same cut. Except mine
was sleeveless.

Lime green. Meaning:
the inside of the lime.

I want you to feel what I feel.
It won't wash off.

Can someone shut that dog up?

44. THE REASON WHY SHE ENTERS THIS TRANCE

He used a photo of Ella Fitzgerald, a glass-framed photo, which is how it came to be called "Ella" in our circle. I'd hang around drinking wine, smoking Bob, and talk to any asshole all night long. Am I saying this in French yet? The guy in regular clothes talking to the guy in chef's clothes before the restaurant opens—isn't he already basically human? He's just made of wood, is that so bad? He has yearnings, he has dreams. Making reference to her "connectivity" beside the giant spools of hose, a flag planted in the border—because. You need to be profoundly numb, is why. The reason why I shot so many pictures is part of my story. I don't know if you can make this out, but it's Mahatma Ghandi talking on the phone.

45. ONE OF THOSE TREES WAS MY TREE

He stood
in the doorway. He sat here.
And the window
was open.

He was a boy once.
He did his best not to bury me.
He said he didn't want me to think
he was doing it on purpose.

46. THE LITTLE MYSTERY OF THE KNIFE

Sometimes he drives to another town.
It isn't clear what "nearby" means.

Their jackets are off. They're almost like lovers.
Maybe this is enough.

He's living within a set of ideas he won't challenge
again in his lifetime. On the other side,
men watching the horse race in the dark.

One day we took a walk in a place we'd never been.
He's a soldier, used to carrying a gun.

"Is this for me? Who am I to you?"
Black water on a sunny day means wind.

47. ALL OUR BONES

All our bones, and the mountains.

Mountains always in the distance.
It's called completion.

I want us to tell people.

900 words and every photograph preceded by a warning.
You've forgotten, I think, but I was guided by your dream.

It has something to do with my father, sure. I understand
the desire. The wavy glass in the door—it all started so long
ago.

I understand the willingness. The keys in the ignition.
Secret things that belong to God.

We used to wonder how old we'd be in heaven. I understand
the trance. Recording angels. The ones that read our deeds.

49. DID YOU TRY TO HURT YOURSELF THIS MORNING?

There is no water on Mars, or
no liquid water
that anyone believes is still there.

So much dust and so much light
upon it. "But, in that light," he said

. . . I can't remember.
To bend the teeth of a permanent displacement?
I think it means fear of strangers.

We have a little bit of choice.
I miss everyone. It's good to have the chance.

43

Where are those who would arm me?

44

—Mainly I remember when it was gone. Lying in bed, trying to
believe I'd ever sleep. Once it was done, I had to get alone. I went
to bed because there was nothing else to do. I'd be too jacked up
to read, and there was no internet back then. Basically, I'd just lie
there thinking *never again.* And that resolution might last a little
while. Until somebody had some, or said "Let's just get a quarter
and split it."

—A quarter gram?

—Yeah. At first, splitting a quarter was something you could do.
You'd get a quarter, then you might get another quarter . . .

There's never enough. That becomes true pretty quickly.

Although, this one time, a couple friends of ours were dealing, mov-
ing fantastically large amounts. They'd be getting these big black
trash bags full of cocaine. Giant bags! I'm not talking about kitch-
en trash bags. The emptied bags would get stashed in a closet to be
scraped down later. But this one time, our friend gave my mother
and me two of these empty bags. Didn't look like that much, but I

scraped down the insides with a credit card (very carefully) and it lasted for days. Maybe three days.

—Three days on what was clinging to the bag?

—It was dust, but for a day or so it really felt like "endless supply." Well, there was just the two of us. And the whole time, we made Christmas ornaments.

—Made them how?

—Out of dough. Salt dough. Then we'd bake them, and paint them. We made tons of them, all different. I still have the George Smiley ornament she made, and one I made of my grandmother, though her arm cracked off at some point. I think that was the most fun I ever had doing coke. Just sitting at the kitchen table, me and my mom, doing lines, drinking tea, making ornaments. After it was gone, we slept for a day and were okay. We were still at the beginning.

I actually had a coke dream last night. I used to have them a lot, now not too often. They're awful. Typically, I'm snorting it off the floor, off a really filthy rug or something, which I never even did in life. But the dreams really bring it back: how you just don't care. About anything. And how, as soon as you start, you're already in a bad mood and all you want is more. After a while, it wasn't even exactly about the high for me. I mainly wanted the feeling of it burning up my nose into my head.

In these dreams, I see it, I don't want it, and I can't resist. And that's how I remember it: I only want a taste! and it's all over. But that one time, making the ornaments? That was fun. And it turned out to be quite a handsome Christmas tree.

45
He's a man again. He said it would be important later.

46
I told you yesterday.

47
I can't.

48
You never know until it happens to you.

49
Even then you don't know.

50. I WAS DRIVING DOWN THE LAKE ROAD

We were heading in opposite directions. I passed her,
then tapped the horn and backed up until she stopped,
and I came alongside her.

Our windows were open. We talked a little.
No one else was on the road.

It was just like any day.

51. FRIENDS FOR LIFE

There are 3 people searching for you.

52. A CAPPELLA

That day?
I was trying

to talk with her,
but nothing came.

We didn't laugh.
I couldn't find her.

Do you like this music?

53. IT'S TEN-TWENTY AND THE SAINT IS WALKING BY

In her set called "every day," bridal veil was a fall
and a search for candles.

Tell me how you want to feel.

The market offers charms for curing fright, bettering
the earth, "attract a lover," but like she used to say:
I'm in the book. Meaning: I'm not here.

Meaning it's a mystery you can't crack.

There's a crime in everybody's past.
Black snow filling up the page.
There's always been a leak.

I didn't trust him. I knew I couldn't. But I liked being with him because there was something . . . He could make me laugh. And we had this physical affinity. I never really could kiss anybody else the way I kissed him. Which made me realize: that stuff—? It doesn't have anything to do with anything.

55. ORDINARY TIME

Put on the veil. Or pull
a portion of your shirt
over your head
and run away.

56. BECAUSE

Fairness isn't natural.

You never see it
in nature.

These pictures are my notes.
I always take a lot of notes.

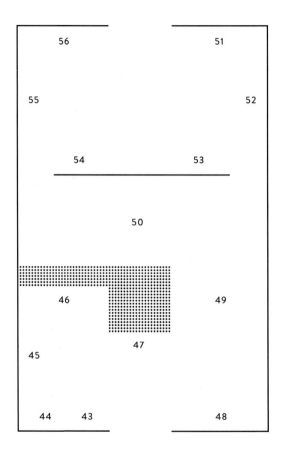

57. BLACK ICE (BECAUSE THEY'RE INVISIBLE)

We have the towels and basins out (the leaks).

At night we hear them running in the walls.

58. THE SMOKER

He's just a person who lives in the building.
He occupies the husband's space in the frame.

We must be able to trust one another.
Public, private—it's just how things are.

It rained. I took a walk around the parking lot
with an umbrella. When I came inside,
a little girl was at the elevator.

She had a kind of shell on her back,
like a turtle shell that held two swords.

She pulled down the neck of her shirt, and showed me
the scrape on her shoulder, where she fell off her scooter.
Yesterday was her birthday.

Does looking at her picture tell you something?

59. THEY ALL WANT TO TRY THE VEIL

Everybody's jealous of the little girl.

Where is she now?
That's her thinking music.

60. CARDBOARD STAR

I wrote down what I wanted to say.
Because nobody will touch it.

Our man fights—it's his second
language. Before he leaves

he sets up a tiny tree on the table.
She wouldn't give a reason.

The children did this.
I think she had a very common reason.

61. ONE NIGHT THE MOON WAS BRIGHT

I watched her through the half-open door.
I was separate, outside myself.
It was my moment.
Snow.
They call it snow. Or noise.
I could hear the river.

62. I REMEMBERED THE OX EYES

She once worked in a supermarket and often her dreams are
in a grocery store fused with some other room, like in her
grandmother's house. She wants so little really.

I watched her walk to the counter,
cut out the bitter green heart.

Brideweed, devil's flax, bread and butter.
To borrow, but not to understand.

I thought she said, "You'll need a secret."

Look at him out there. Nature
is an awful, awful thing.

63. TICKLE MY ARM

I had a life—black
and blue, it swelled.
I couldn't—I was reading my own name.

The monkey in the basement is a metaphor.
But I remember thinking *why won't he just stop
being bad?* So he wouldn't get hit.

The camera glances at his photographs, his notes.
A man's body? Weighs as much as a man.
Outside, the dog. On a rope.

Spending time in the story is the point.
And of course it's Christmas.
1963.

57
Because the old words are no good.

58
I knew once but I've forgotten.

59
Guided by a cloud by day and a fire by night.

60
This is my first picture

61
of how I feel. Stand back.

62
You have to stand back

63
to see it.

64. WHAT IT MEANS TO BE A STRANGER

I was back on the farm. I felt though that I was not really there but remembering, because new elements were present. I saw some sheep cut in half but they were hollow. I swept out a tiny building that didn't used to be there, which led to a system of tunnels underneath the ground. I just wanted to be alone in the tiny place I'd swept, but I could hear people coming up through the tunnels. I seemed to have nowhere else to go, and then, miraculously, I had the thought: "If this is remembering, I could try to forget," and with that I woke up.

65. BRIDEWEED

It was yesterday and my sister
was getting married. She was afraid
of the fire. She signed a document they said
would save her. The church was dim and modern.

A lot of people were already there. I didn't see anyone
I knew. I fell asleep, got up, made soup, tried to
answer your mail. Is it easier to look at
now? Yes, in a way.

Faith
is necessary, almost not
quite to the day, so quiet
we could hear the petals fall.

Of his blindness, of what calls he answered,
she is the trace.

Are we free from this fragrance?

Any couple's private life means what.
The way they keep their house, their animals,
the way they do sex?

It doesn't work for me.
It doesn't work for my sister.

I found a chalk eraser I could use to erase myself.

I loved rubbing it all over me, the way it felt, then walking
around—just some smeared chalk dust no one noticed.

66. I'M TRYING TO MAKE A PICTURE OF THE DARK

The tools, the ladder, the dust, the lake—
he told me nobody knew
what to photograph.

He felt that he had made some bad decisions
and that it was hard to make good ones.

"The first conversation
must be the impossible one."
I didn't have notes for that.

We had a map to start with. *Daddy,
look what I drew.*

67. SPOONS HAVE A TASTE

It's what I'm supposed to want.
I want it.
In a way.

I'm just glad I don't have to live there,
you know,

with the ox
and the monkey.

The camel
passed me in the hall.
Narrow as the eye of a needle.

—I talk to her. All the time.

—What do you talk to her about?

—Mostly I just *interact* with her. You know, I'll bring her forward and I'll say, "Okay . . . I know." [laughs] She'll just be looking at me. She'll be sending me mental signals. Like "Get to work" or "Don't forget about me." She has her different moods. Like sometimes she's sort of funny and sometimes she's sad.

—When she sends you "mental signals," is she speaking to you? Is she talking? With words?

—Not exactly.

—But you're translating it into words?

—I talk to *her*. She's just a doll. She can't talk. It's like talking to a ghost, in a way. I mean, ghosts can't really talk to you, they don't exist.

—You've had some experiences, though, haven't you? With things that don't exist, or figures that appeared . . . ?

—I have. And I don't know what that means. I have no idea. I used to believe in things more.

69. BLACK SNOW

I thought we might be friends. Or we were friends but
who we turned out to be was disappointing.

She walks to the corner of the field. One of those cold
bright days you remember from childhood.

The past, nothing.
New people, nothing.

She sees him but she doesn't know him.
She's wearing his coat.

70. SOME PEOPLE USE A SENTENCE

When I told her, she said: "You can't tell me this."
I said okay.

The table had been laid.

64
You saw the field, the tree, the tunnels and the roots under the
ground, the empty house, the fence. You had a good interpreta-
tion. I remember feeling it was good.

65
I hope you didn't blame me much.

66
Within quotation marks: Dan Beachy-Quick
(*The Conversant* interview with Randall James Tyrone)

67
I like my stolen spoons and knives the best.

68
—Why do you call her the client?
—Because I work for her.

69
By "ghost note" he meant a note not played but felt.

70
I wonder what she'd say if I reminded her of that.

You were there, we were all there, at the table. The light! I suddenly recognized the past. I wanted so much to explain.

Remember—? I was trying to say.

You didn't know what I was talking about. It was all from the future. The room started filling up with strangers.

I got up finally, somebody was calling my name. The hallway was stinking with dead fish. I thought of all the times I didn't die.

You, your burning hand, your open broken read-my-mind—I cut my thumb knuckle trying to teach myself to peel a potato like my grandmother would. In long, curving strokes. Toward the body.

72. LITTLE OAK

We were going to move to Reno.
Our imaginary daughter had become real

and there was somebody there
who could help her.

Heard it on TV: "I call it
with your life involved."

"Reno?"
you said.

(Gradually cease to be an acorn at all?)

Her little foot.

73. BEFORE THE CHANGE, THREE DAYS

A man walks away from a building as another man walks in. They don't speak. The arriving man is in security. Last week, after he said "no pictures," he asked me to leave the factory parking lot. There will be another person. Not yet clear who that could be.

74. HYACINTH

My dead wife in her blue suit.
And me in a brown suit, running.

There was more.
I could see her breath.

We were coming out into the open.

75. INSTEAD OF A CHORUS, CERTAIN WORDS

Giant face
Small face
Long ash

Clocks
wrapped in plastic,
things that didn't happen.

People dancing outside—in coats!

She sees it.
Who she'll have to be.
There are only so many stories.

76. BECAUSE WE LOVE THE UNCROSSED DISTANCE

Box marked *papers to take to the motel.*

Why?
To remember who I am?

One: "That the soul
could be created, with desire." Fourteen years pass.

Two: "Like music . . . like mathematics . . .
the accumulated" (something else, crossed out)

Three: "Little lights coming up on the horizon."
Mountain, maple leaf, world without end.

How does a person slip
from one life to another?

Do you have a car?

77. RED FOR MEMORY

A statue is raised—
a little piece of wind: Don't forget us!

Why not distruth? Unappearance?
The pictures are tacked up to help me think.

The dream is represented by people at a distance.
What would I tell a friend?

She's a doll, she dies in childbirth, she becomes a man.
She's a detective. She's working, all the time.

71

Title: Hexagram 27 of the *I Ching*, "a picture of an open mouth."

72

Maybe everyone has faith in something. We found a bracelet.
A bracelet with her name.

73

Sun / The Gentle (The Penetrating, Wind), Hexagram 57, nine in the
fifth place: "No beginning but an end. Before the change, three days.

74

After the change, three days."

75

People have a good side.

76

Before today, only a particle.

77

Broken off.

78. 0.99999999=1

I keep trying to get to the sink to wash my face,
but something prevents me.

Someone
I can't remember.
I can't remember who they used to be.

I'm the same person. It's the same day.
Or the next day. What day were you looking for?

79. THEORY OF THE QUALITIES OF FEELING

arms baby bride brother / building camera car color
daughter dreamer father flower / ghost girl Jesus ladder
lake leak Mars math / Mike mother mountain picture
prayer / river / shutter / sister / veil

"A weak white light is not a grey light."

—*There's a sense of landscape in your work.*
—*Yeah, I like memory.*

80. WHAT TO DO WITH THE WILL TO BELIEVE

Like Jesus said: "Let it happen."

Hyacinths? for Christmas?
Or maybe it's some other day.

We bought and tried to wear new clothes,
held in our hands the pink quartz stone
that would open our hearts.

Whatever happened to divine
discontent? Longing
as the basis of self-discipline.

He took the camera, in the end.
When the tools were gone.

You'll see so many things.

81. BLUE FOR LOYALTY

The boat is out too far. We'll most likely sink before we reach land, and I'm spending so much time on duty! Should I have sex? A sandwich?

Maybe later. Before we go down. If we do.

82. "YOU'RE SLEEPING ALL DAY AGAIN"

I know. I know what I said yesterday.

I had to close my eyes for just a second.

83. WHAT DOES A BABY REPRESENT IN DREAMS?

We had her out on a beautiful blanket,
out near the sea. A moment of sun.

Those flowers?
We used to call them snowballs.

I like the blue ones.
We lost her here.

84. "HOW THEN ARE SOULS TO BE MADE?"

He carries her things to the car.
Finally he cries.

78

What makes sense depends on the light.

79

"The uncanny, Freud tells us, is concerned with 'the theory of the qualities of feeling.'" (Nicholas Royle, *The Uncanny*). Within quotation marks: Ludwig Wittgenstein (*Remarks on Colour,* #218). In italics: part of an exchange between Doug Aitkin and Mark Bradford (#49 in Aitkin's film *Station to Station*).

80

His notes or what we know as his teachings.

81

That the soul could be our home, later.

82

Can the days be long enough to get me there?

83

I wanted the baby to behave but she said: "I can't love now."

84

Title: John Keats to George and Georgiana Keats
in the spring of 1819.

85. THE ART OF ARMS

Look at yourself and realize who you are.
If poetry is a place to think,
where they bring the drowned of the river.

The song begins.
Such a tiredness! Another song.
Tiny bullets for a tiny gun.

—When you miss her now, what do you miss?

—Oh. The understanding that we shared, at one time. A million times. I've never been so joined up mentally to anyone as I could be with her. What does preternatural mean? That's the word that comes to mind. It was a preternatural connection. A psychic told us once: "It's almost like an out-of-body point you guys have. Where you're free to look at things together." That felt true. But [long pause] so many things happened. I knew her my whole life. And for a long time it seemed like she was the only one who really knew me, or ever would.

Here it is: *preternatural. Beyond what is normal or natural.* So, yeah, that is the word. *Autumn had arrived with preternatural speed.* Near the end, she kept asking, "When can we go home?" "We are home," I'd say, sometimes. Sometimes I'd say, "Soon."

87. SNOWBALL, STORM AT SEA, TRIP AROUND THE WORLD

And is there a chair? In the open?
I was on my way to somewhere else.

Fourteen years ago, you told my fortune.
You took me to the train. We talked in the car.

"I'm in your group," I said. "What do we stand for?"

88. I HAD TO THINK OF SOMEONE I LOVED

He has 40 pages on the land
and the wind. In that light, he says,
the hardness of the self disappears.

Is "yourself" within you
or something that moves through you
or the way you act?

Or is it more like
something you collect.
Not everything is a lie.

It's amazing how you can begin
to forget
people.

I hear them slipping away.

89. A PILE OF STICKS STOOD UP

Drove until it felt like time to stop.

Short night.
Breakfast here starts at five.

The dog can hear him so he thinks I should be able to.
Drink more talk more whatever he wants. She won't bark.
I trained myself to trust my intuition.

Oh we were talking . . . Our grandson's neighbor
got a divorce and when they split up, neither one
could take the dog.

In the dream where he appears, are these clothes ours?
Nakedness in this sense is blankness.

Friendly? Oh yes, very friendly. Throws the ball all day.

Bombs. "Maybe they won't be atomic."

I close my eyes against the light. "But look," he says, "it's God, smiling." He's so pleased. It's a picture on the dresser: of God, God the Father, holding something in His hand and looking like He's figured something out.

Patience. "Is this where we live?"

There was a child. I knocked him down a few times, accidentally. He was holding something unwieldy. I picked him up then and told him I was "not a good helper." But I was "a friend."

This idea of progress—that we're headed toward some goal or rest or understanding—can you shake it off and stay alive?

I didn't go to the window.
I was unable to pursue the thought.

91. I SAW MYSELF NAKED BY MISTAKE

All my life, I wanted to be closer
to God. To know the shapes of trees.

To know the longitude and latitude
with certainty, amidst erasure
of landmarks.

But. It's a different alphabet.
To save yourself or save someone you love.
Then they take your car.
My voices?

They're mostly just the smoker's TV.
I saw it last night, in his window,
glowing like a lung.

85

For a long time, I didn't know what to say. And of course I didn't
want to say it.

86

There was a place near water.

87

We all traveled together. And I believe we shared one hope.

88

The print on paper will certainly be lost.

89

A pile of sticks stood up and seemed
like a little dog, made of sticks and driftwood.

90

It walked toward the fire, then into it, and lay down,
relaxing—suddenly, profoundly. You said (because I was crying):
"It's not alive." "It has volition!" I said, or thought.

91

My prayer is changing.

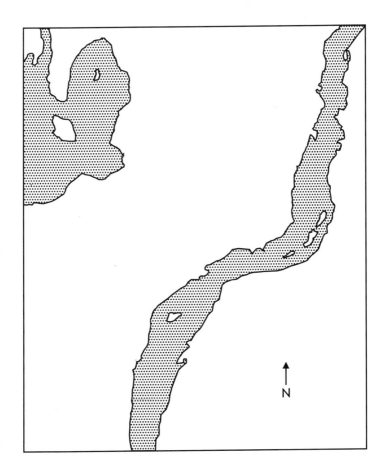

Knowing yourself and knowing the future—it's all part of the same thing, right? We do sometimes know things we shouldn't be able to know. It happens all the time with dreams. I think our lives are out in front of us a little. Endings are a problem, and what to tell. Have you ever died in a dream? Real endings aren't something you choose.

You know the idea "If you want to change the world, forgive someone"? It's not just because we lose everything. Years pass, you find another truth.

I smell my grilled cheese burning. I eat it anyway and think about my childhood, when I would only eat toast black. Actually I don't think about my childhood, I think about that toast. I put another sandwich on, and burn it on purpose.

93. OF A YEAR NOT GIVEN

Like Jesus said: "Stand back."
But why wouldn't he let her touch him, really?

Because he'd been dead? Because he was leaving?
Because, at last, he was another kind of being?
Was it for her sake or his own?

I had a life. There is someone I think of,
drawing with my hair on the shower wall.

He was speaking in a quieter world
and people came to listen, people walking.

But this photo is proof he was with you.

All pictures are incomplete.

Sometimes sleep.
How we remembered who was who.

94. ARE YOU HAPPY, BABY?

There are only so many stories. Maybe twelve.

Secret? Secret from who?
She starts in.
She's tired already.

—When I think of that day, I think of the moment when you
fell. And how we tried to put it behind us, even as I lifted
you up. [Thinks: *I'm a girl. I can stand this way for hours.*]
Couldn't I be closer to people?

—No. I don't know. I don't think so. Maybe. Maybe from
the corner of your eye.

Distant sound of men pounding stakes into the ground.
[Thinks: *I am a soldier.*]

Some leaves never let go.

—But don't they always fall in the end?

—I don't know. Presumably.

—Are they dead? Even if they still hang on?

—Depends. On your definition. But yes.

95. TINY LADDER

Imagine things are moving all the time.

The waves have traveled from the fault
to where you are.

The paper, the sticks, the trees
with their shadows.

Everybody wakes up together.

Everything is gonna be okay,
she said.

I thought the room
was breathing

but it was me.

96. WORK ON WHAT HAS BEEN SPOILED

Remember when that girl whose dog's name was Boo gave us a jar of corn relish? Homemade. It was delicious! And we asked her if her dog was named for Boo Radley and he was.

A funeral? But that would be too public.

I wouldn't want to say because I wouldn't think anyone would care. Or I wouldn't want to stand up.

Shape of a cross on the wall. The shape
of a cross where the cross used to be.
Songs based on songs.

Maybe this is what you mean when you say it's better not to be in touch?

97. ONE HAND, $5

People want to know about love. And money. Or "Yes, the world will soon acknowledge . . ."

She sensed my interest, I guess. I was walking by—it was a summer thing. Something good would happen.

Maybe they waited too long to set out. It's always far away— the birthplace, the big famous tomb. Or maybe—it's just a picture in my mind, people walking in the moonlight.

I didn't go to any trouble. It came to me, it was no trouble. People can't help it. They try—to make up a new reason. Then they say it's natural.

We can't forget—she's told us everything already.

I liked when she tapped my fingers at the end and said, "That's it."

I dreamed Doc Watson died and his wife went temporarily blind in her grief. I was traveling somewhere and happened to meet her. I took her hand as she climbed into an open-bed wagon—wooden, huge, with wooden benches on two sides. I sat with her then, and we fell in love in a way. I think we both felt that our attraction would last only as long as her blindness. But I woke up before she could see again, so I don't know.

That's my other life following me. Woman driving a pale green pickup, hood secured with a length of chain. Two little kids sitting with her. No front plates, mirrors built out from the sides. Her elbow resting in the open window, beaded necklace swinging from the rearview—two strands, pink and blue. I think she's singing. Can't tell if she wants to pass. This is her chance.

IN MEMORY OF B

Shhh . . . that pain
woke me up again

You'd made a book

A Book of Little Pins
you called it

I cried over your book of little pins
it was so beautiful and you   were lost

no one knew where

Following a sound?

Sometimes in the middle of the woods the singing stops.

PRINTED IN CANADA

AHSAHTA PRESS
2017

JANET HOLMES, DIRECTOR

PATRICIA BOWEN, *intern;* LINDSEY APPELL; MICHAEL GREEN;
KATHRYN JENSEN; COLIN JOHNSON; MATT NAPLES